INCREDIBLE SPACE

Space Robots

by Steve Kortenkamp

Reading Consultant:
Barbara J. Fox
Reading Specialist
North Carolina State University

Capstone
press

Mankato, Minnesota

Blazers is published by Capstone Press,
151 Good Counsel Drive, P.O. Box 669, Mankato, Minnesota 56002.
www.capstonepress.com

Library of Congress Cataloging-in-Publication Data
Kortenkamp, Steve.
    Space robots/by Steve Kortenkamp.
    p. cm. — (Blazers. Incredible space)
    Includes bibliographical references and index.
    Summary: "Discusses information about space robots within recent years as well as the future
of space robots" — Provided by publisher.
    ISBN-13: 978-1-4296-2322-3 (hardcover)
    ISBN-10: 1-4296-2322-5 (hardcover)
    1. Space robotics — Juvenile literature. I. Title.
TL1097.K67 2009
629.47 — dc22   2008029830

Editorial Credits

Abby Czeskleba, editor; Ted Williams, designer; Jo Miller, photo researcher

Photo Credits

Alamy/PHOTOTAKE Inc./Michael Carroll, 14
AP Images/Ric Francis, 13
Getty Images Inc./Dream Quest Images Touchstone Pictures, 23
NASA, 5, 6, cover; John Frassanito and Associates, 26; JPL, 11, 18, 20–21, 28–29; JPL/DLR, 17;
    JPL-Caltech, 9; JSC, 24
Shutterstock/argus (technology background), throughout; hcss5 (minimal code background
    vector), throughout

1 2 3 4 5 6 14 13 12 11 10 09

Table of Contents

chapter 1

Helpers in Space

A space shuttle docks with the *International Space Station*. Long robot arms pull equipment out of the shuttle. The robot arms attach the new equipment to the space station.

International Space Station

a place for astronauts to live and work in space

The space shuttle *Discovery* docks with the *International Space Station*.

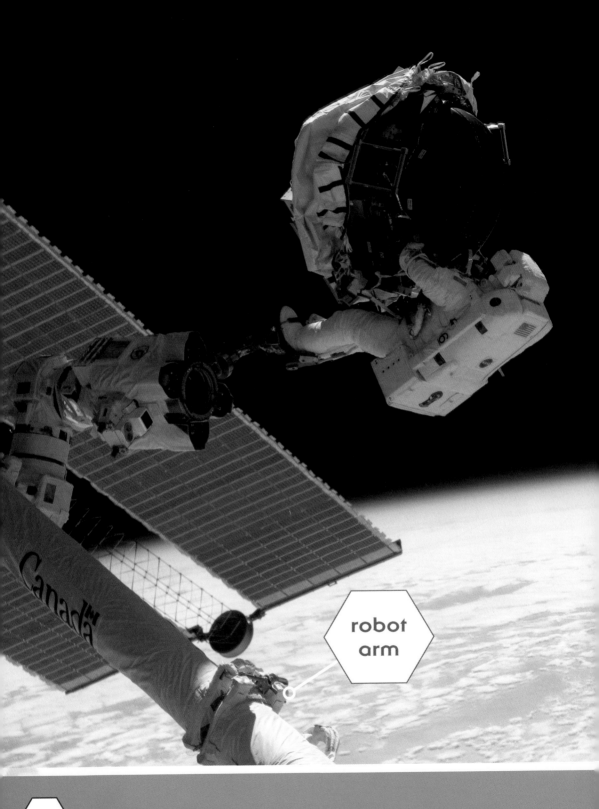

robot
arm

Space robots help astronauts with hard jobs. A robot arm can hold an astronaut steady. It can also move large equipment into place.

astronaut

a person who is trained to live and work in space

Space robots explore **planets**. Robots can also go to other places that astronauts haven't explored. Robots and astronauts may one day discover faraway places together.

planet
a large object that moves around a star

A robot explores rocks on Mars.

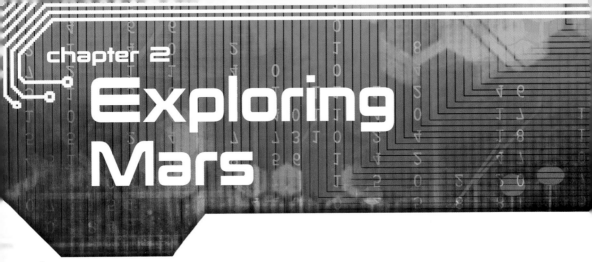

chapter 2

Exploring Mars

Two **rovers** have been exploring Mars since 2004. They send pictures of Mars back to scientists on Earth.

rover

a small vehicle that explores objects in space

The two Mars rovers are called *Spirit* and *Opportunity*.

Scientists tell the rovers where to explore. They use special glasses to look at the pictures from Mars. The scientists then send new directions back to the rovers.

There may have been water on the surface of Mars.

Today, Mars is a dry planet. It has many **dust devils**. Pictures from the rovers show that Mars may have been a wet planet.

dust devil
swirling winds full of dust that look like a small tornado

INCREDIBLE FACT
Scientists think the water on Mars may be frozen underground.

chapter 3
Frozen Adventures

In the future, robots will travel to many new places in space. Robot submarines can melt through ice on one of Jupiter's moons. Water is underneath the ice. Robots may look for **aliens** in the water.

alien
a creature not from Earth

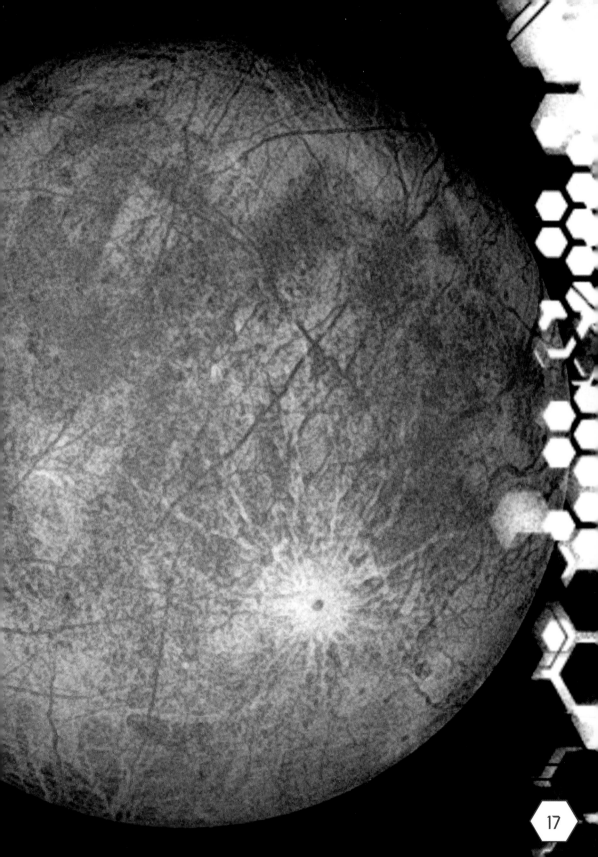

17

A spider-bot may one day explore
the Moon and other places.

Robots may also explore icy **comets**. Scientists may send small robots inside comets. The robots will learn what is frozen in the comets.

comet

a ball of rock and ice that circles the Sun

INCREDIBLE FACT

Some robots move like animals. Snake-bots slither and spider-bots crawl.

camera

solar panel

Diagram

antenna

wheel

chapter 4

Robot Teammates

Someday, astronauts will travel to Mars. But before they do, robots will build bases on the planet. Astronauts will use the bases to explore Mars.

INCREDIBLE FACT

A day on Mars is about as long as a day on Earth.

The 2000 movie *Mission to Mars* showed what bases may look like when astronauts visit Mars.

Some robots look and act like astronauts. These robots are called **robonauts**. Robonauts will carefully repair equipment in space.

robonaut

a robot that looks like a human

26 Astronauts will bring robonauts when they travel to Mars.

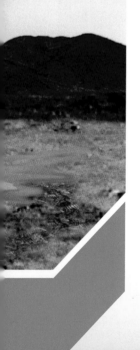

Astronauts and robonauts will explore space together. They may even do some of the same jobs. Just imagine what astronauts and robonauts will find on Mars.

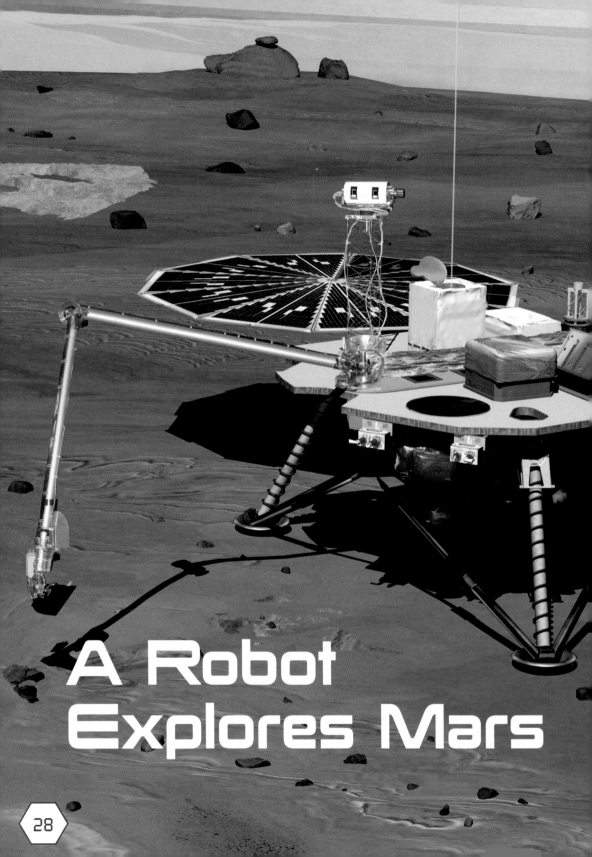

A Robot Explores Mars

Glossary

alien (AY-lee-uhn) — a creature not from Earth

astronaut (AS-truh-nawt) — a person who is trained to live and work in space

comet (KOM-uht) — a ball of rock and ice that circles the Sun

dust devil (DUHST DEV-uhl) — swirling winds full of dust that look like a small tornado

International Space Station (in-tur-NASH-uh-nuhl SPAYSS STAY-shuhn) — a place for astronauts to live and work in space

planet (PLAN-it) — a large object that moves around a star

robonaut (ROH-bo-nawt) — a robot that looks like a human; robonauts can do many of the same jobs as astronauts.

rover (ROH-vur) — a small vehicle that explores objects in space.

space shuttle (SPAYSS SHUT-ul) — a spacecraft that carries astronauts into space and back to Earth

Read More

Grego, Peter. *Voyage Through Space.* QEB Space Guides. North Mankato, Minn.: QEB, 2007.

Hyland, Tony. *Space Robots.* Robots and Robotics. North Mankato, Minn.: Smart Apple Media, 2008.

Kortenkamp, Steve. *Space Probes.* The Solar System. Mankato, Minn.: Capstone Press, 2008.

Internet Sites

FactHound offers a safe, fun way to find educator-approved Internet sites related to this book.

Here's what you do:

1. Visit *www.facthound.com*
2. Choose your grade level.
3. Begin your search.

This book's ID number is 9781429623223.

FactHound will fetch the best sites for you!

Index